FEARLESS!
STUNT
PEOPLE

TIME
FOR KIDS

Jessica Cohn

Warning!
All the stunts in this book have been performed by professionals. Never try these stunts at home. Ever!

Consultants

Timothy Rasinski, Ph.D.
Kent State University

Lori Oczkus
Literacy Consultant

Eric Bryson
Stunt Performer

Eliza Coleman
Stunt Performer

Based on writing from
TIME For Kids. *TIME For Kids* and the *TIME For Kids* logo are registered trademarks of TIME Inc. Used under license.

Publishing Credits

Dona Herweck Rice, *Editor-in-Chief*
Lee Aucoin, *Creative Director*
Jamey Acosta, *Senior Editor*
Heidi Fiedler, *Editor*
Lexa Hoang, *Designer*
Stephanie Reid, *Photo Editor*
Sandy Phan, *Contributing Author*
Rachelle Cracchiolo, *M.S.Ed., Publisher*

Image Credits: Cover & p.1 Altaf Qadri/
EPA/Newscom; pp.11, 18, 18–19, 26–27, 28, 29 (top), 32, 32–33, 36–37, 46–47, 48–49, 52–53, Alamy; p.48 Associated Press; pp.8–9 Bettmann/Corbis; pp.4, 6–7, 15 (bottom), 24 (bottom), 29 (bottom), 40 Getty Images; pp.38, 39, 41 Jen Decker; pp.9, 10–11, 14 Library of Congress; p.25 David Allio/Icon SMI/Newscom; p.42 Isack Saasha/SIPA/
Newscom; pp.12–13, 20–21, 30–31, 34–35, 44–45, 50–51 (illustrations) J.J. Rudisill; p.46 (illustration) Timothy J. Bradley; All other images from Shutterstock.

Teacher Created Materials

5301 Oceanus Drive
Huntington Beach, CA 92649-1030
http://www.tcmpub.com

ISBN 978-1-4333-4941-6
© 2013 Teacher Created Materials, Inc.
Printed in Malaysia
Thumbprints.22064

TABLE OF CONTENTS

Pulling Stunts 4

Early Stunt Work 9

On Wheels 17

Fight Club 26

Blaze of Glory 36

Falling Hard 42

The Art of Action 53

Glossary 58

Index 60

Bibliography 62

More to Explore 63

About the Author 64

PULLING STUNTS

An army of warriors runs across a patch of jungle. They dodge small explosions and flying spears. Their leader swings on a long vine over their heads. With a kick to the head, the enemy is down. The director yells, "Cut!"

The working conditions for stunt people range from uncomfortable to dangerous. Very little about this career is a safe bet. But that doesn't bother those who do it. Stunt work is for people who enjoy activity and seek challenges. This job is unique, exciting, and filled with adventure. The stunt community is also a social bunch. These highly talented people challenge one another to create extreme effects. But every day, they keep it safe and professional.

- Why would someone want to be a stunt performer?
- How do stunt people train to be successful?
- How do stunt performers avoid injuries on the job?

5

Stunt performers train to survive action that would kill normal men and women. They study with experts and attend stunt schools. Students start by learning to fall, faking a fight, and rolling down the stairs. More advanced classes teach students how to look like they're being blown back in an explosion. Others teach the art of driving at high speeds, falling through glass, and surviving a fire. The students' training lets them walk away from a burning building or take a blow to the head. Every stunt is designed to be as safe as possible, and teachers show students how to calculate risks.

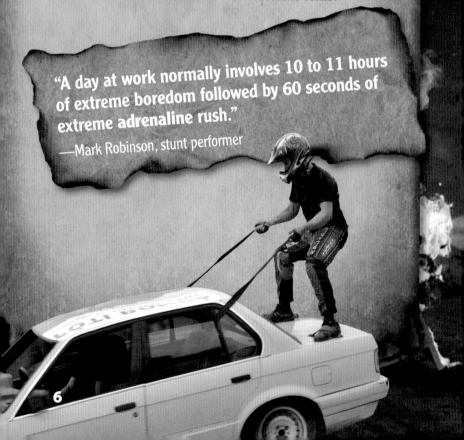

"A day at work normally involves 10 to 11 hours of extreme boredom followed by 60 seconds of extreme adrenaline rush."
—Mark Robinson, stunt performer

Personality Profile

Stunt performers tend to be the people who tore up their backyards as kids. They often did **martial arts** or other contact sports. This challenging work requires intelligence, courage, and plenty of practice. It's the opposite of a desk job, and that's just the way successful stunt performers want it. Do you have what it takes?

Can you plan for risks?

Are you a team player?

Are you coordinated?

Are you physically strong?

In 1920, pioneer stunt performer Ormer Locklear stood on top of a plane flying 90 miles per hour.

That's the Ticket

Circuses have always featured stunt people in their acts. When movie directors wanted to show something daring, such as someone flying high on a rope, circuses supplied people with the right training.

EARLY STUNT WORK

The pioneers of stunt work were pure **daredevils**. Some even lost their lives for fame. In the early 1900s, **aviation** was a new field. Pilots traveled across the country, selling rides in their airplanes. They were called *barnstormers* because they set up shop in farm fields.

The most popular fliers, such as Ormer Locklear, did daring tricks. Locklear was called the King of the Wing Walkers because he walked on the wings of his moving plane. Then, Hollywood came calling. In 1919, he was the first person to be filmed moving from a car to a plane while both were in motion. The next year, he died in a crash scene.

Variety of Skills

Vaudeville was a form of entertainment popular in the late 1880s to early 1900s. The shows included magicians, animal trainers, dancers, and **acrobats**. As movies gained popularity, the vaudeville shows died out. But many performers found their way to Hollywood—and to stunt work.

Slapstick Stunts

For years, films were black and white, short, and silent. Filmmakers couldn't record action and sounds at the same time. Sometimes, music and a few captions were added after filming. Most of the early stunt actors were comedians. They got laughs with **sight gags**. The actors were slapped around, run over, and suffered other mishaps.

Slapstick is a physical form of humor. Buster Keaton was one of the best slapstick actors. He was raised in a vaudeville family. He trained for stunt work by performing in his family's rough-and-tumble stage act. Keaton later performed on Broadway and then in films.

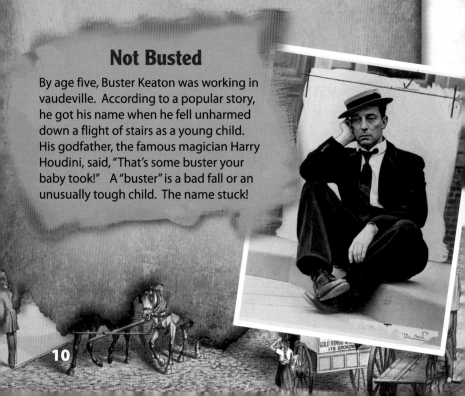

Not Busted

By age five, Buster Keaton was working in vaudeville. According to a popular story, he got his name when he fell unharmed down a flight of stairs as a young child. His godfather, the famous magician Harry Houdini, said, "That's some buster your baby took!" A "buster" is a bad fall or an unusually tough child. The name stuck!

On Broadway

Broadway is a long street in New York City. In the mid-1800s, many theaters opened on and near Broadway. Today, just as Hollywood is the capital of the American film industry, Broadway is the theater capital. To perform "on Broadway" means an actor performs in a major big-budget play.

Comedy Trio

The Three Stooges were a group of funny film pioneers. They were known for their cartoon-like slapstick, silly sound effects, and funny hairstyles— frizzy curls, a bowl cut, and a bald head. The comedy team appeared in almost 200 films from 1934 to 1970.

11

DIG DEEPER!

Slapstick Step by Step

Physical comedy often involves people getting smacked around. The audience enjoys laughing at the characters' bad luck. However, performing a successful gag means no one actually gets hurt. Slapstick stunts are planned and timed carefully to avoid injury.

The Slap

1

2

3

The Setup
The actor keeps her fingers loose.

Perfect Timing
The other actor turns his head in line with the hand's movement, just barely avoiding the slap.

Sound Effects
He claps his own hands at time of "impact."

The Knockout

The Setup

The comedian turns carelessly while holding a long pole.

Perfect Timing

The innocent bystander falls down a split second before the pole hits his head.

Sound Effects

He slaps the ground to make a crashing noise.

Safety Tricks

A gag is all about creating the illusion of an accident or violence. Moe of The Three Stooges didn't poke his friends right in the eyes but on the brows above the eyes. Physical comedians may also use weapons and objects made of plastic or foam in their acts. These dull, soft items are less likely to hurt people.

Remember!
Never try this at home.

Modern Cowboys

As movies became more complex, so did the stunts. When Western movies became popular, performers needed to do tricks on horses. Many of these performers, such as Tom Mix and Yakima Canutt, came from **rodeos**. Today, stunt people still often come from rodeos. They may also start in extreme sports or motocross racing.

Many of the best performers go on to become **stunt coordinators**. They direct stunts. They also plan where to place cameras and other equipment. They know exactly how to make audiences gasp.

In the Mix

Tom Mix, "King of the Cowboys," was a star in silent Westerns. He grew up riding horses, working on a ranch, and performing in rodeos. In 1910, he had his first part in a film. He went on to make hundreds of movies.

Canutt Can

Yakima Canutt won many rodeo championships. He was famous for being able to jump over the back of a moving horse and land in the saddle. In 1966, he won an Oscar for building the stunt industry.

The work professional drivers do often comes with a warning: Do NOT try this yourself.

Resume Reel

Many stunt drivers have a website where they list their racing accomplishments and work in film and television. They also post photos and videos of their stunts and races. People looking for a stunt driver often ask for a clip reel, or video collection, of the driver's best work. Getting the job means letting potential employers see them in action.

ON WHEELS

Today, stunt performers specialize in different types of stunts. Professional drivers create some of the most exciting action on screen. They drive to mountaintops and cliff edges in TV commercials. They jump cars over other cars. In the movies, stunt drivers make chase scenes look easy.

Professional drivers take cars to the limits of what they can do. They gain skills by driving countless miles on racecourses and off roads. Their training helps them control a storm of natural and automotive forces. Stunt drivers are masters of **hand-eye coordination**. And they know their vehicles on wheels inside and out.

Training Wheels

Drivers learn **mechanics** in driving school. They study steering and hand placement. Experts teach them how to judge road conditions. They test their side vision and repeat basic movements, such as steering sideways through cones. Making a **180°** **turn** look good on film takes a lot of practice.

Action!

What makes a car scene exciting? As expected, police chases and car races put audiences on the edge of their seats. But often, the first time a stunt is performed is considered the best. Moviemakers continue to offer new stunts. Some recent films feature **drift racing**. In these action-packed movies, teams of drivers circle and skid on all wheels, trying not to run into each other. One popular film includes a scene in which a car speeds through a spiral ramp. The car goes sideways!

Actor Jason Statham drove his way to fame in blockbuster action films. As a kid, he trained in martial arts and diving.

Making It Pay

The **median annual salary** for stunt work varies widely. The performers belong to the Screen Actors Guild (SAG). Members of SAG require a minimum payment of a few hundred dollars a day. But assignments may only come every few months. Stunt performers who rise to the top regularly make more than $100,000 a year.

Risks Involved

Though fun to watch, stunt driving can be a real pain. The cars are powerful, and speeds are high. Getting bruised, feeling sore, and suffering headaches is common. Though deaths are rare, stunt drivers find it hard to get **disability insurance**. So they take their lives into their own hands in more ways than one.

A stunt driver crashes through a pile of debris.

Turn by Turn

Stunt drivers must be able to precisely control cars. They learn everything about cars and what cars can do. In this way, a stunt driver lets the car do the work naturally instead of forcing it to do tricks. Check out how drivers can get a car that's supposed to move forward and backward to drift sideways!

The stunt driver pushes in the clutch.

The driver yanks up the hand brake to countersteer.

The driver flicks the steering wheel to steer the car into a slide.

Pressure on the **throttle**, or gas pedal, controls the angle of the drift.

For some scenes, a driver's hands must be at the eight and four o'clock positions on the wheel to stay out of the camera frame.

21

Tricks of the Trade

Being a stunt driver requires a variety of skills. Drivers need to handle many kinds of vehicles. They must also be able to perform a range of tricks, from drifting to high-speed car chases, but the most important trick is becoming well known. Many stunt drivers hire **agents** to help them get started. They begin as movie **extras**. Some join SAG. The group helps stunt drivers meet other people in the film industry and learn what jobs are available. They also try to get the attention of directors, producers, and stunt coordinators.

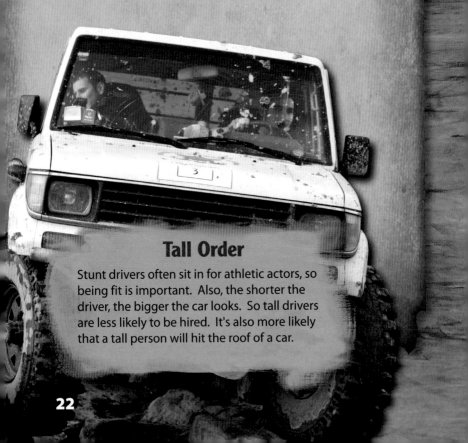

Tall Order

Stunt drivers often sit in for athletic actors, so being fit is important. Also, the shorter the driver, the bigger the car looks. So tall drivers are less likely to be hired. It's also more likely that a tall person will hit the roof of a car.

Uphill Drive

This career is an uphill drive. For every driver with a job, there are hundreds without one. And most drivers do most of their driving in their 30s. When they are older, they often need to move on to other roles, such as stunt coordinator or trainer.

Speedy Sisters

Debbie and Donna Evans paved the way for women in the driving world. Debbie (left) was in the driver's seat during a famous action scene when a small car drove under a moving semitruck.

Who's Who

Tanner Foust is one of the most successful professional drivers. He has won the gold medal at the **X Games** three times. He was twice declared the winner of the Formula Drift championship. Foust is best known as the host of TV programs such as *Top Gear USA* and *Battle of the Supercars*. However, his body of work as a movie stunt driver is also impressive. He drove in many popular action films and commercials.

Close Calls

On his website, stunt driver Tanner Foust shows videos of himself driving close to cliffs and boulders. Each video begins with a warning. No matter how exciting the work seems, no one should try it on his or her own. This is highly skilled work that requires the right kind of training.

FIGHT CLUB

It's hard to beat the excitement of driving, but professional fighting is a top **contender**. Many fighters are masters of martial arts and weapons work. Others box or fight fist to fist.

The goal of a fight scene is to make it as dramatic as possible. Making it feel real is key to hooking the audience. The best fights are filmed with little or no editing. In some movies, the action also needs to reflect the time period of the film. A fighter in a western acts a certain way in a saloon fight. A fighter in a martial-arts movie uses different moves.

The Dragon

Bruce Lee was one of the biggest names in martial-arts movies. They called him The Dragon. He invented Jeet Kune Do, a type of fighting that focuses on the philosophy behind martial arts. His intense fight scenes thrilled audiences worldwide and continue to inspire martial artists and moviemakers today.

Combat Classes

One of the first things drama students learn is how to fake a fight on stage. The actor turns slightly away from the audience, thumps his or her own chest, and falls as if injured. But the camera films a fighter from all angles. Movie stunt people need to keep it real for film.

Chan, The Go-To Man

For top-notch stunt fighting, look no further than Jackie Chan. He is an actor and a **choreographer**. He is a singer and a stunt performer, as well as a world-class comedian.

Born in 1954 in Hong Kong, Chan was trained in martial arts and acrobatics. When he was a teen, he became a stuntman for Bruce Lee. In 1971, he starred in his own movie. Since then, he has performed in many popular action comedies. His sense of timing, which serves him so well when fighting, also helps him get laughs.

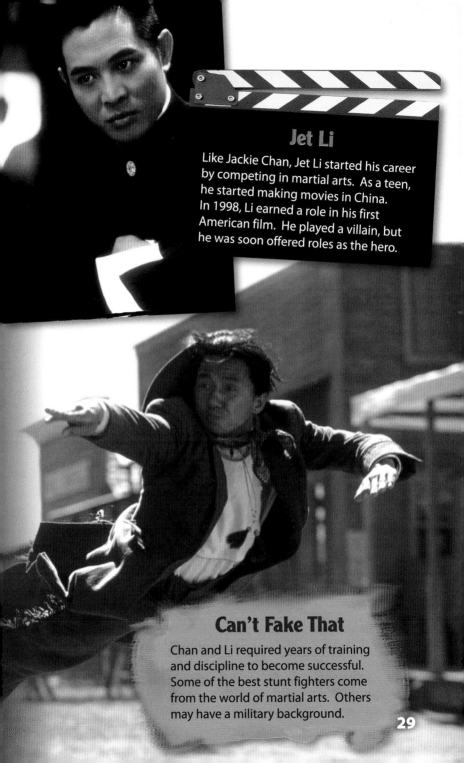

Jet Li

Like Jackie Chan, Jet Li started his career by competing in martial arts. As a teen, he started making movies in China. In 1998, Li earned a role in his first American film. He played a villain, but he was soon offered roles as the hero.

Can't Fake That

Chan and Li required years of training and discipline to become successful. Some of the best stunt fighters come from the world of martial arts. Others may have a military background.

DIG DEEPER!

Pow! Zow! Wow!

In one of his most famous action scenes, Jackie Chan fights crooks in a mall. The scene is filled with broken glass, flying trash cans, and exploding lightbulbs. Movie fans love to watch this scene. It shows why Chan, perhaps more than anyone, has made Hong Kong fighting films popular around the world.

Chan jumps over a railing on to a moving escalator, where he rips into a bad guy.

Even well-planned stunts can go wrong. During filming, Chan burned his hands badly while sliding down a two-story pole. The lights were too intense and made the pole hot.

The hero turns a clothes rack into a deadly weapon.

Chan flips a man backward into a glass display case.

31

Digital Effects

Moviemakers can now use **computer-generated imagery (CGI)** to show wars and disasters. Computers can show fights without placing people in danger. This means the work is safer, but there are fewer jobs for those willing to take risks. Some battle scenes feature thousands of fighters. However, most of these fighters are digital. The scene may only employ a few live stunt actors.

Keeping a fighting career alive is hard. It takes discipline. Fighters need to hit their marks. They need to exercise to keep up with the action and danger. To compete for jobs, they must **promote** themselves.

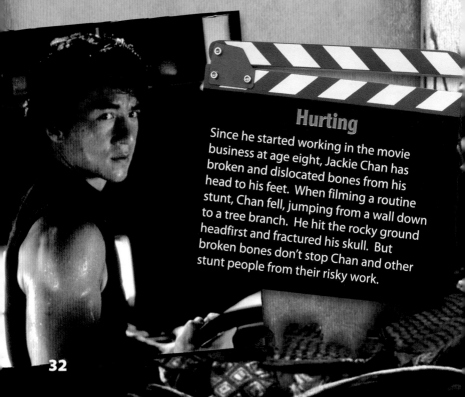

Hurting

Since he started working in the movie business at age eight, Jackie Chan has broken and dislocated bones from his head to his feet. When filming a routine stunt, Chan fell, jumping from a wall down to a tree branch. He hit the rocky ground headfirst and fractured his skull. But broken bones don't stop Chan and other stunt people from their risky work.

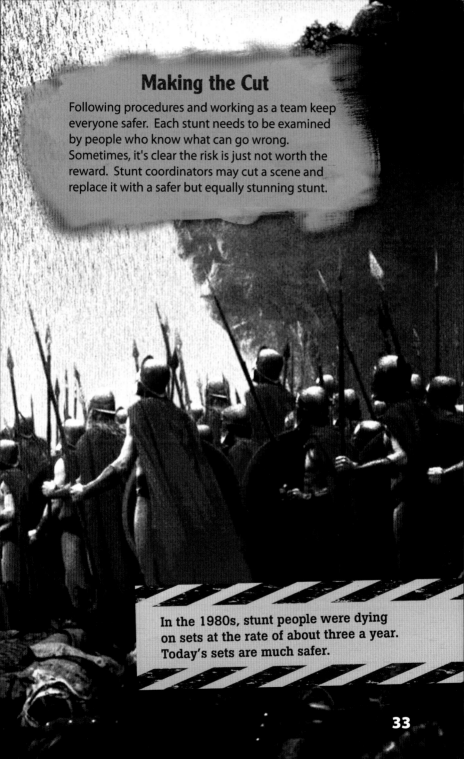

Making the Cut

Following procedures and working as a team keep everyone safer. Each stunt needs to be examined by people who know what can go wrong. Sometimes, it's clear the risk is just not worth the reward. Stunt coordinators may cut a scene and replace it with a safer but equally stunning stunt.

In the 1980s, stunt people were dying on sets at the rate of about three a year. Today's sets are much safer.

Warrior Workout

Stunt performers must be strong and fit. Most work out every day. In addition to training for stunts, they also do activities such as yoga, running, tennis, or mountain biking.

A stunt performer practices different punches and kicks with bags or a partner.

The workout begins with a 15-minute warm-up of stretches.

Next come 10 minutes on the trampoline. The trampoline helps stunt actors improve their balance.

STOP! THINK...

Why do you think stretching is the first step?

Why is it important to repeat the same movements over and over?

Do you think safety is as important during training as it is during filming?

Training with weapons or practicing fight scenes helps a stunt performer prepare for the moment when the director calls "Action!"

The last step is a cooldown with core exercises such as crunches and planks.

BLAZE
OF
GLORY

A popular action film featured a memorable scene on a pier. The scene begins with a gunfight between the bad guys. A plane flies overhead. A good guy drops gasoline out of the plane and shoots at it. The pier bursts into flames, and the bad guys fly into the water.

To make this scene realistic, the stunt crew set the pier on fire several times. It was the kind of blazing action that also blew up online message boards. Film fans who were used to computer-made effects declared that the pier scene was an example of good old-fashioned movie action.

Don't Get Burned

Fire stunts are in a terrifying category all their own. These specialty stunts require intense training and planning. The people who work with fire wear special hoods, gloves, and other safety gear. The movie may be make-believe, but the fire is real and dangerous. Fire will eat its way through nearly anything.

Too Hot to Handle

Within this category of stunts, there is often a need for **pyrotechnics**. This work can be literally too hot to handle. It takes planning and follow-through to create and control an explosion and the fire that follows. The scenes must be rehearsed thoroughly.

Record-Setting Fire

In 2010, Colin Decker set a Guinness World Record for the longest full-body burn. He "burned" from head to toe for three minutes and 27 seconds and lived to tell about it.

Remember!
Never try this at home.

Special Forces

In 2004, fire experts Colin Decker and Dustin Brooks joined forces to create the company Fire 4 Hire. They share many years of experience in the stunt business. The company has also developed its own fire gel, which when applied to skin and set on fire makes flesh look as if it's burning.

Decker and Brooks share many credits. Their movie stunts range from fireballs and burning cavemen to fire-breathing mythical monsters. The two are often called in as **consultants** when a script calls for a big burn.

Colin Decker

Dustin Brooks

Studying Safety

Stunt performers study how fire behaves. They learn which parts of the body are most sensitive to heat and how special clothing works to protect those areas. They also learn about fire safety and first-aid information.

Truly Scary

In the late 1930s, during the filming of *The Wizard of Oz*, Margaret Hamilton, the woman who played The Wicked Witch, was burned. A trap door **malfunctioned**, and she was left facing fireworks. Her face and hand were badly burned, and she was hospitalized.

Any use of fire is filled with risk. When Decker and Brooks set someone on fire, it's a well-planned operation. The "victim" wears a flame-fighting garment, which is much like long underwear. There is a special suit of clothing over that, and then the gel. Needless to say, no one should even think of doing this alone. Even with these precautions, the gel can heat up more than the human body can bear.

The Wicked Witch (Margaret Hamilton) threatens Dorothy (Judy Garland) in a scene from *The Wizard of Oz*.

Fire Crew

When someone burns in a scene, there are many safety workers standing by with fire extinguishers. There is also a pool of water close by. There is nothing safe about working with pyrotechnics or any kind of flame.

Life Science

Stunt work seems to require fearlessness, but the best people in this line of business have a healthy fear of fire. They approach their work as scientists would, and they consider everything that might go wrong. Special gel helps protect performers, but they still need to be aware of its limits.

Seriously! Never try this at home.

FALLING HARD

Fear runs through any kind of stunt like emotional electricity. By playing with the audience's fears, the performers produce a feeling of **awe**. That is why falling is yet another stunt specialty. Most people fear high places and falling. Stunts that involve falling thrill audiences.

Falling takes special training, acrobatic skill, and grace under pressure. A body that is falling speeds up as it goes down. Performers must learn to use tools that slow down the effect or soften the blow. For the longest falls, performers use air bags and long elastic ropes called **decelerators**.

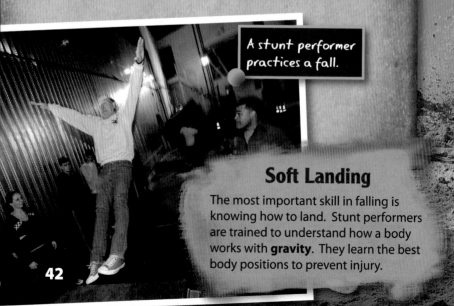

A stunt performer practices a fall.

Soft Landing

The most important skill in falling is knowing how to land. Stunt performers are trained to understand how a body works with **gravity**. They learn the best body positions to prevent injury.

Going Vertical

Stunt performers study how to fall from extreme heights. They practice doing headers, the face-off, and the back fall. They learn exactly what gear to use for each fall.

Falling and Flying

A fall that lasts only a few seconds on screen may take hours of planning. Flying, flipping, and fighting in the air requires equipment that moviegoers never see. Here is a behind-the-scenes look at what goes into some of the coolest gravity-defying stunts.

Setting Up a Fall

A stunt person leaps off a platform.

Spotters stand by to watch for problems. They are trained to step in if an accident occurs.

A large air bag cushions the stunt person's fall.

Rigging Rundown

A stunt person is strapped into a harness and a wire rig.

Filming against a green screen lets moviemakers add special effects later.

A crash pad prevents injury in case of a fall.

Remember! Never try this at home.

Close to Falling

One of the most memorable jumps of all time occurred in a James Bond film. The famous spy dropped more than 700 feet into a building guarded by bad guys. In reality, the stunt double, Wayne Michaels, performed the fall with the help of a **bungee cord**. The fall was filmed at a dam in Switzerland. To make sure the stunt man didn't hit the side, moviemakers built an **extension** along the top of the dam. That gave him a wider area to work with.

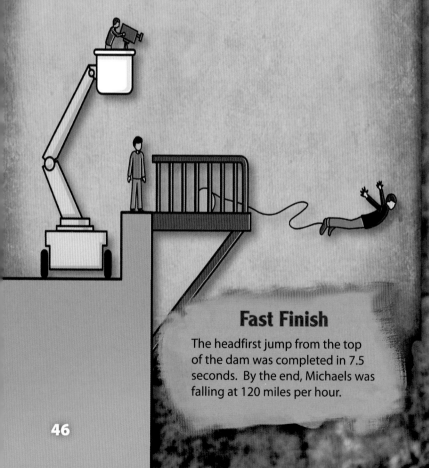

Fast Finish

The headfirst jump from the top of the dam was completed in 7.5 seconds. By the end, Michaels was falling at 120 miles per hour.

Stunt coordinators must consider weather and wind speed when planning outdoor falls.

Breaking Fall

The jump that Wayne Michaels did for the Bond movie broke a record in moviemaking. It was the longest bungee jump off a structure.

Daring Dar

Dar Robinson was a leading movie daredevil. His first major stunt was a hundred-foot leap in 1973. He held 21 stunt records. In 1980, he dropped 900 feet from the Canadian National Tower, a building with a flared base. He factored in the winds around the tower. Hanging from a thin cable, Robinson came within 200 feet of hitting the ground.

Robinson was known for planning his stunts carefully, but he died at age 39 while filming a stunt. He successfully flew off a motorcycle and into a ravine. Then, he got back on the bike. Later, during a simple chase, he **inexplicably** drove off a cliff before he could brake and prevent a fall.

Robinson drops to a trampoline hanging from a helicopter flying 300 feet above the ground.

Tall Tale

Dar Robinson rehearsed his stunts carefully. When testing the cable for the Canadian jump, it broke. He had to adjust his plans before going ahead with the stunt.

Expecting the Unexpected

Until the day he died, Robinson had never broken a bone. The incident that killed him was totally unexpected. The main stunts had been completed for the day, and the medical staff had been sent home.

Awarding Action Heroes

The Taurus World Stunt Awards are the Oscars for stunt performers. To be part of the Taurus academy and eligible for an award, a person needs to have a lot of experience performing and a recommendation from a current member of the academy. Winning a Taurus is a high honor and a sign of success.

An action hero shakes hands with his stunt double.

Support for Stunt Work

Part of the academy's mission is to provide compensation for performers who are hurt on the job. The Taurus World Stunt Awards Foundation gives money to injured stunt people. The academy offers help if an accident prevents a stunt person from working.

At the stunt awards, death-defying acts are performed throughout the night.

Awards

* Best Fight
* Best Fire Stunt
* Best Overall Stunt
* Hardest Hit
* Best Work with Vehicle

"Knowing is not enough; we must apply.
Willing is not enough; we must do."
— Bruce Lee, actor and martial artist

THE ART OF ACTION

For a stunt person, no two days are the same. The job may call for a thrilling car chase, a violent fight scene, or being set on fire. These daring performers must be experts in a wide range of skills. In this line of work, there is no room for error. A successful stunt calls for the perfect mix of calculated risk, extreme skill, and showmanship. And the best performers study with the pros that came before them.

Stunt School

Stunt schools offer workshops or training sessions that last from one day to three weeks. Some schools have online classes. They teach brave students to perform bold stunts. Class subjects include tumbling, breaking glass, weapons, and fire safety. But the best way to learn the business is from the pros. Most stunt performers learn from each other. They train with experts and pass their skills on to new performers.

Lights! Camera! Action!

When the training is over, it's time to perform. Stunt people spend hours training, working out, and practicing. An entire stunt crew may spend days creating a few seconds of action. Their work keeps audiences on the edge of their seats, fearing for the performers' lives. So the next time you see a heart-stopping scene, remember these masters in the art of action made it possible. That is *real* movie magic.

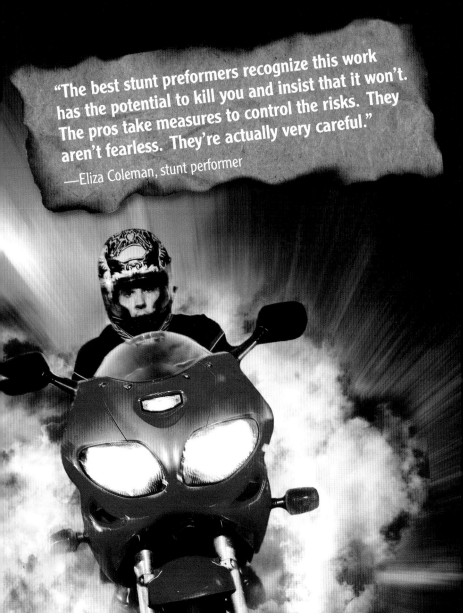

"The best stunt preformers recognize this work has the potential to kill you and insist that it won't. The pros take measures to control the risks. They aren't fearless. They're actually very careful."

—Eliza Coleman, stunt performer

The Real Deal

Meet Mark Donaldson, the president of the Stuntmen's Association of Motion Pictures. Donaldson has worked on popular TV shows and blockbuster films including *Lost* and the *Pirates of the Caribbean* franchise. His credits include stunt actor, coordinator, driver, and fighter. He sat down with writer Jessica Cohn to talk about his career.

Jessica: How did you become a stunt performer?

Donaldson: I planned it for three years before moving to California. . . . This was a dream, and I pursued the dream against what everybody told me. I was told, "You can't do that."

Jessica: What is a working day like?

Donaldson: In one movie, we're lying in sand as dead bodies, and the sand is 106 degrees. Or you jump into a river to do a fight, and the water is 47 degrees. [Basically], you show up. There's a bit of socializing. A plan is made, usually by the stunt coordinator. . . . Or sometimes they call, and you don't know what you're doing. You just know to bring your bag of pads to protect your body.

Jessica: What advice do you have for people attracted to this job?
Donaldson: Learn all you can from working stunt people. Remember, whatever the mind can conceive, the body can achieve. But always be safe. Always plan for the unexpected.

Jessica: Anything else?
Donaldson: There are a few excellent driving schools. But the best thing to do is to get to know people in the industry—the ones who know what they're doing—and let them teach you. This is a business of getting along with people.

GLOSSARY

acrobats—people who perform feats that require a high degree of muscle control, such as balancing, tumbling, and swinging from things

adrenaline—the substance that raises blood pressure and prompts the body to act quickly

agents—people who act or do business for another person

aviation—the operation of aircraft such as airplanes and helicopters

awe—a mixed feeling of fear, respect, and wonder

bungee cord—a cord or rope of stretchy material, which absorbs shocks

choreographer—a person who plans dance and similar moves in performances

computer-generated imagery (CGI)—pictures created by computers

consultants—people who give professional advice

contender—a competitor who wishes to become a champion

daredevils—people who are bold, sometimes reckless, and enjoy taking chances

decelerators—special ropes and wires that slow a fall

disability insurance—guaranteed payment if injured on the job

drift racing—a motorsport in which drivers oversteer to make the car slide or "drift" sideways

extension—a section or part added to make something larger or connected

extras—people hired to act in the background of a scene

gravity—the pull of any object with mass

hand-eye coordination—the control of eye movement with hand movement

inexplicably—that which cannot be explained

malfunctioned—worked incorrectly or did not operate normally

martial arts—the art and sport of combat and self-defense

mechanics—the details of the way something works or is done

median annual salary—the amount of money made yearly by someone in the middle of the range

180° turn —a stunt in which a car does a 180-degree turn at the end of a skid, turning halfway around

promote—to advance or to advertise

pyrotechnics—the art of making and using fireworks

rodeos—performances and contests featuring calf roping and similar events; places where these events take place

sight gags—comic effects produced by visual means rather than spoken lines

slapstick—comedy stressing horseplay and humorous violence

stunt coordinators—the people who plan and direct stunts in movies and TV

throttle—a pedal for controlling speed

vaudeville—a form of entertainment that featured many types of acts including dancers, musicians, comedians, trained animals, jugglers, and magicians

X Games—a sports event that features extreme sports

INDEX

acrobats, 9

air bag, 42, 44

barnstormers, 9

Battle of the Supercars, 25

Broadway, 11

Brooks, Dustin, 39–40

bungee, 46–47

California, 56

Canadian National Tower, 48

Canutt, Yakima, 14–15

Chan, Jackie, 28–32

China, 29

choreographer, 28

circus, 8

clutch, 20

computer-generated imagery (CGI), 32

crash pad, 45

daredevils, 9, 15

decelerators, 42

Decker, Colin, 38–40

director, 4, 8, 22, 55

Donaldson, Mark, 56–57

Dorothy, 40

Dragon, The, 27

drift racing, 18

Evans, Debbie, 25

Evans, Donna, 25

Fire 4 Hire, 39

Formula Drift, 25

Foust, Tanner, 25

Garland, Judy, 40

Guinness World Record, 38

Hamilton, Margaret, 40

hand brake, 20

harness, 45

Hollywood, 9, 11

Hong Kong, 28, 30

Houdini, Harry, 10

James Bond, 46–47

Jeet Kune Do, 27

Keaton, Buster, 10

King of the Cowboys, 14

King of the Wing Walkers, 9

Lee, Bruce, 27–28, 52

Li, Jet, 29

Locklear, Ormer, 8–9

Lost, 56

martial arts, 7, 18, 26–29, 52, 54

mechanics, 17

Michaels, Wayne, 46–47

Mix, Tom, 14

Moe, 13

motocross racing, 14

motorbike, 15

New York City, 11
Oscar, 15, 50
Pirates of the Caribbean,
    56
pyrotechnics, 37, 41
rig, 45
Robinson, Dar, 48–49
Robinson, Mark, 6
rodeos, 14
Screen Actors Guild
    (SAG), 18, 22
sight gags, 10
spotters, 44
Statham, Jason, 18
stunt coordinators, 14,
    22–23, 33, 56
stunt double, 46–47, 50
stunt drivers 16–17, 19–20,
    22, 24–25

Stuntmen's Association of
    Motion Pictures, 56
Switzerland, 46
Taurus World Stunt
    Awards, 50
Taurus World Stunt Awards
    Foundation, 51
Three Stooges, The, 11, 13
throttle, 21
Top Gear USA, 25
trampoline 34
vaudeville, 9
Westerns, 14
Wicked Witch, 40
Wizard of Oz, The, 40
X Games, 25

BIBLIOGRAPHY

Cummins, Julia. *Women Daredevils: Thrills, Chills, and Frills.* **Dutton Juvenile, 2008.**

At a time when they were expected to stay at home raising their families, these remarkable women performed some outrageous acts. Read this book to learn about stunts that would make anyone's heart stop.

McClellan, Ray. *BMX Freestyle (Torque: Action Sports).* **Bellwether Media, 2008.**

Executing stunts on a bike requires skill and precision. Learn about the different equipment riders use and the tricks they do to win competitions.

Mello, Tara Baukus. *Stunt Driving (Race Car Legends).* **Chelsea House Publications, 2007.**

High-speed chases, colliding cars, explosions—stunts like these take hours of practice and require perfection. You may see only a few scenes with adrenaline-pumping action, but the life of a stunt person is exciting every day. Find out more about the art of stunt driving in this book. Be warned: This career is not for the faint of heart.

Weintraub, Aileen. *Stunt Double (High Interest Books).* **Children's Press, 2003.**

Explore one of the most dangerous jobs around. Stunt performers must be precise and not afraid to get hurt. Jumping through flames, rescuing hostages, diving off a cliff—no two days on the set are exactly alike.

MORE TO EXPLORE

Stunt Driving Games

http://www.agame.com/games/stunt_driving/stunt_driving.html

Find out what it would be like to be a stunt driver. Take your pick of vehicles and master these courses.

StuntKids.com

http://www.stuntkids.com/index.asp

Take classes and learn the business of stunt performing from the experts. Here, you'll also find pictures and resumes from kids currently trained to perform stunts as well as pictures of them in action.

International Stunt Association

http://www.isastunts.com

This site has pictures, stunt reels, and a gallery of members. See if you can spot any of them in the next action movie you watch.

Bruce Lee Biography

http://www.biography.com/people/bruce-lee-9542095

Learn more about this iconic stuntman, from his early life as a child actor to his role teaching kung-fu to the masses.

ABOUT THE AUTHOR

Jessica Cohn grew up in Michigan. She has a bachelor's degree in English and a master's in written communications. She has worked in educational publishing for more than a decade as a writer and an editor. During that time, she has researched many careers, but stunt performance is surely among the most fascinating. She is married and has two sons. Her family is based in New York state.